DEVELOPING COMPREHENSION

First Book

Alan Lynskey

Margaret Stillie

Illustrated by Corinne Burrows

STANLEY THORNES

Contents

Introduction

Developing Comprehension is an attempt to clarify and to develop the many skills involved in the real comprehension of language.

The Barrett taxonomy, on which the series is based, presents five main categories of comprehension.

1 Literal comprehension: answering questions by direct reference to the text. These answers are usually explicitly stated in the passage.

2 Reorganisational comprehension: classifying, collecting and organising information explicitly stated in the passage. The information may be collected from more than one source.

3 Inferential comprehension: detecting information implied in a passage. This demands thinking and deduction beyond what appears in the passage.

4 Evaluative comprehension: interpreting and evaluating the writer's assumptions or intentions, often by comparison with the reader's own experiences or opinions.

5 Appreciative comprehension: responding to a passage with enjoyment, and with an awareness of its language usage and emotion.

Obviously these skills are not clear cut and separate. There is a considerable overlap between categories. Certainly the higher-level skills – the ability to appreciate and evaluate written material – require the child to exercise literal and re-organisational skills in order to reach decisions.

Techniques
Developing Comprehension uses a variety of techniques to develop reading skills:

Prediction
Predictions are vital to the reader's active involvement in what he or she is reading. In the exercises we ask "What do you think happens next?" In the classroom children should be asked to discuss their predictions and the evidence which supports them. Teachers can give more practice in prediction by breaking a passage into sections and asking "Where do you think this is happening?" "What will so-and-so do next?" "What will happen then?" When the next section is read, the children can evaluate and revise their predictions in the light of what they have learnt.

Cloze texts
These are passages with words omitted, which children are asked to supply. Often there is no right or wrong answer. The child is asked to supply the best word he or she can think of which contributes to the meaning and the feeling of the passage. If the chosen word can be justified, then it can be judged as right. Sometimes the missing word will be determined by the structure of the

sentence, and there will be little argument. But in every case, discussion of alternatives and reasons for choices is vital to the learning process.

Sequencing and ordering

The child is asked to place events in order or sequence. Technically, he or she will need to be able to pick up indicator clues (next, but, etc.) which relate one paragraph to another, and then comprehend the underlying pattern of a passage – to understand across whole paragraphs the development of events. These passages are especially valuable when used in small group discussion. Some whole-class oral work will complete the lesson.

Evaluation

The teacher needs to have clear purposes of evaluation. *Developing Comprehension* is designed to evaluate and improve children's ability to read and fully comprehend. Answers, therefore, should be evaluated initially by the way they display the child's understanding and appreciation of what he or she has read. Classroom discussions should begin with meaning, before looking at how to record that meaning in written English.

The work produced, written or oral, indicates to the teacher the strengths and weaknesses of each child. Programmes of work can be developed to cater for the weaknesses of individuals or groups of children.

The evaluation of responses to cloze texts and prediction and sequencing exercises will be oral as comparisons are made and reasons put forward as to why one choice is better or worse than another. Discussion sessions are crucial in helping children to see what they have missed in their reading, and they encourage purposeful re-reading, which is a vital higher-level skill.

Marking and assessment

The responses or answers a child makes are a starting point for teaching, not a final assessment. Even a totally inappropriate answer will provide a basis on which to work.

The level of difficulty of a passage in relation to a child's reading level must be taken into account in any assessment. No child can be expected to make an evaluation or appreciation of a passage he or she can read only with difficulty. But teacher expectation is a significant factor in pupils' attainment and should not be pitched too low.

We have chosen passages of high literary merit, including the best writers of contemporary children's fiction. We hope that children will be encouraged to read more of the work of the writers they have enjoyed.

ALAN LYNSKEY
MARGARET STILLIE

Jacki '84

6

The kitchen

1 What has the mother been doing?
2 How old do you think the girl is?
3 What is the girl doing? Do you ever do that?
4 What do the family keep on top of the cupboard?
5 How do you think the milk got spilt? What makes you think so?
6 Do you think the mother has seen the spilt milk? What will she do when she does?
7 What is the weather like outside? Write the things in the picture which tell you about this.
8 Why do you think Mother is wearing wellingtons?
9 What is Mother going to do next?
10 Why do you think the cat is looking in through the window?

Why hares have long ears

Once upon a time a hare made friends with a goat, and they started living together and sharing everything.

One day the goat said to the hare:

"Let's build a house!"

5   "Let's!" answered the hare.

So off they went into the forest for some logs. They came up to a tree and the goat said:

"I'll knock this tree down!"

"You'll never!" said the hare.

10   "Oh, but I will. I'll just show you!" answered the goat. And he took a long run, and went Crash! into the tree with his horns, and the tree fell down.

And the hare said to himself:

"So that's the way to knock trees down! Now I shall be
15 able to do the same." And they came to another tree, and the hare said:

"I'll knock this tree down!"

"You'll never!" said the goat.

"Oh, but I will. I'll just show you!" answered the hare.

20   And he took a long run, and went Crash! into the tree with his forehead!

And the tree still stood where it was before, but the hare's head had gone right into his shoulders.

The goat saw that he must get the hare's head out from
25 his shoulders, and he caught hold of the hare by the ears and began to pull. He pulled and pulled, till at last the hare cried: "Stop!"

But the goat still went on pulling. He pulled the hare's

head back to its proper place, and his ears went way out
30 from his head!

And that's why hares have long ears.

Picture Folk Tales
Valery Carrick

1 What did the animals need logs for?
2 How did the goat knock the tree down?
3 Why do you think hare said "You'll never!" (line 9)?
4 Why did hare cry "Stop!" (line 27)?
5 Why do you think goat went on pulling? What happened when he did?
6 What did hare think when he saw goat knock down the tree? Was his idea a good one?
7 Write down what happened when hare butted the tree. Why didn't that happen to goat?
8 Write in your own words why hares have long ears.
9 Make up a story of your own to explain 'Why elephants have long trunks'.

The beech tree

Rabbit, Goat, Tortoise and Puppy were taking a friendly walk together, when they came to a tall beech tree.

Goat stopped and looked up. "What a splendid view of the whole countryside one would get from the top of that
5 tree!" he said. "Upon my word, I could almost wish that I'd been born a squirrel or a monkey!"

"Pooh!" said Rabbit. "It's easy enough to climb to the top of a tree!"

"I bet you ten pence you couldn't do it," said Puppy.
10 "And so do I!" "And so do I!" said Goat and Tortoise.

"Right," said Rabbit. "All agreed?"

"Yes, yes, all agreed," said Goat and Tortoise and Puppy.

"Right", said Rabbit again. "There's a ladder in Grand-
15 mother's garden. If the three of you will be good enough to fetch the ladder, I'll be up at the top of the tree in a twinkling."

"Oh, but Rabbit," laughed Goat, "we didn't agree that you should climb up with the help of a ladder!"
20 "Nor did we agree that I would do it without the help of a ladder," said Rabbit.

And so the bet was called off.

Oh Really, Rabbit!
Ruth Manning-Sanders

1 Make up a different title for the story.
   Draw a picture of each animal in the story.
2 What were the animals doing?
3 Why did Goat stop?
4 Why did Goat say he would like to be a squirrel?
5 Why did the other animals think Rabbit couldn't climb
   the tree?
6 How did Rabbit trick the other animals?
7 What happened at the end of the story?
8 Did the animals quarrel about the bet or do you think
   they stayed friends?
9 Do you think the ending is fair to everyone?
   Give reasons for your answer.
10 Do you like climbing trees? Why?
11 Which animal did you like best? Why?

Penny and the Captain

Penelope Adeline Willington the Third, called Penny for short, is a penguin. She is first mate on a sailboat named 'The Silverfish'. Mr Jenkins, the Captain, is a walrus. Together they have great fun, and many adventures.

The sun sparkled on the water. Penny kicked off her sandals, threw her feet up on the rail, and said, "I'm not budging".

"Neither am I," said Captain Jenkins. And they didn't
5 move. They sipped lemonade with wild mint leaves. Penny felt a cool breeze. Darkness spread over the sky. Great puffs of clouds rolled in, and it began to pour.

"It's a thunderstorm!" cried Penny. "Oh, rats! Our whole day is spoiled." They packed up and ran inside. Outside the
10 waves were high. Drops of rain splattered the deck, making rainbows in the puddles. Penny tried to count them. "What should we do now?" wondered Penny.

"There's plenty to do," said Captain Jenkins.

"Let's go out in the rain." They played hide and seek.
15 They blew soap bubbles. They splashed in the puddles, and tried to catch raindrops in their mouths.

When they got cold, they went in and drank hot chocolate and apple cider spiced with cinnamon sticks. They read aloud to each other. Everyone curled up and
20 became very sleepy, as The Silverfish rocked in a gentle rhythm.

When the day was over, Penny turned to Captain Jenkins and sighed, "Of all the places we've been, going nowhere was the most tiring of all."

25   "I know," yawned the captain. And they said "Good night."

Penny and the Captain
J.B. Zalben

1 What were the penguin and the walrus doing when it began to rain?
2 What games did Penny and the Captain play in the rain?
3 What three things happened to the weather just before the rain fell?
4 Write down the words that tell you Penny is not pleased about the rain.
5 Find these words in the passage

    sparkled (line 1)   budging (line 3)   sipped (line 5)
    splattered (line 10)   spiced (line 18)

    Write down what you think they mean. Look them up in your dictionary and see if you were right.
6 Why did Penny and the Captain go in from the rain? Why do you think they went outside again?
7 What do you think helped everyone to fall asleep?
8 Do you think Penny and the Captain had a good day? Give reasons for your answer.
9 Draw a picture of The Silverfish. Write its name on it.
10 Have you ever been caught in the rain? Write a story about what happened.

Going swimming

Look at these pictures. They are all about going to the swimming baths. There is one piece of writing for each picture. Read the writing, then write down the number of a picture and the letter of the piece of writing which matches it.

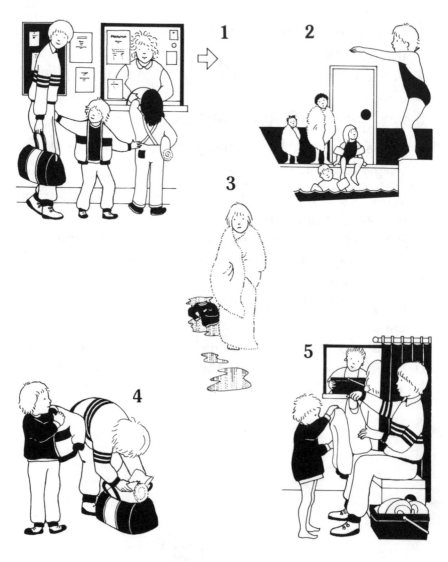

A It's fun in the water. I can swim all the way across the pool. I'm learning to dive now, but it takes a lot of practice.

B Today we're going to the swimming baths. When we have got everything we need we set off.

C The worst part of going swimming is getting dry. I can never get my socks on properly, my hair drips all over me and I always drop something on the wet floor.

D The baths is a new building. The lady behind the cash desk is very slow. She takes ages sorting out the money and the tickets.

E The lady in the changing rooms is much quicker. She gives us a basket to put our clothes in and we get changed.

Now put the sentences in the right order. Choose the writing which begins the story. Write down the letter next to it. Do the same for the others, until you come to the end of the story.

The wormy spaghetti

Mr and Mrs Twit were especially horrible people. They liked to play terrible tricks on each other . . .

Mrs Twit sneaked out into the garden and dug up some worms. She chose big long ones and put them in a tin and carried the tin back to the house under her apron.

5   At one o'clock, she cooked spaghetti for lunch and she mixed the worms in with the spaghetti, but only on her husband's plate. The worms didn't show because everything was covered with tomato sauce and sprinkled with cheese.

"Hey, my spaghetti's moving!" cried Mr Twit, poking
10   around in it with his fork.

"It's a new kind," Mrs Twit said, taking a mouthful from her own plate which of course had no worms. "It's called Squiggly Spaghetti. It's delicious. Eat it up while it's nice and hot."

15   Mr Twit started eating, twisting the long tomato-covered strings around his fork and shovelling them into his mouth. Soon there was tomato sauce all over his hairy chin.

"It's not as good as the ordinary kind," he said, talking with his mouth full. "It's too squishy."

20   "I find it very tasty," Mrs Twit said. She was watching him from the other end of the table. It gave her great pleasure to see him eating worms.

"I find it rather bitter," Mr Twit said. "It's got a distinctly bitter flavour. Buy the other kind next time."

25   Mrs Twit waited until Mr Twit had eaten the whole plateful. Then she said, "You want to know why your spaghetti was squishy?"

Mr Twit wiped the tomato sauce from his beard with a corner of the tablecloth. "Why?" he said.

30 "And why it had a nasty bitter taste?"

"Why?" he said.

"Because it was *worms!*" cried Mrs Twit, clapping her hands and stamping her feet on the floor and rocking with horrible laughter.

The Twits
Roald Dahl

1 Why didn't Mr Twit see the worms on his plate?
2 How did Mrs Twit explain the moving spaghetti?
3 What two complaints did Mr Twit have about the food?
4 How did Mrs Twit carry the worms back from the garden?
5 Why did she choose big, long worms?
6 What does the passage tell you about Mr Twit's table manners? Write out the words that tell you most?
7 Find these words in the passage
   sneaked (line 1)   sprinkled (line 7)
   poking (line 9)   flavour (line 24)
   Write down what you think they mean. Look them up in your dictionary and see if you were right.
8 What did Mrs Twit call the spaghetti? Do you think this was a good name for it? Why? Think of some other names she could have used.
9 If you wanted to play a trick on someone, to do with food, what would you do?

The miller, the boy and the donkey

Do you know the story about the miller and his son, who took their donkey to market to sell him?

Some of the words have been missed out of this story. Choose the word you think fits the story best. Write down your word, with the number of the blank space next to it.

They brushed his coat and combed his mane. He . . .1. . . so smart and clean the miller decided to carry him to . . .2. . . to save him from dirtying his feet on the way.

They had . . .3. . . gone very far before they met a farmer. He burst out . . .4. . . when he saw them. "How silly you are," he cried. "Fancy carrying a . . .5. . .! Why he should be carrying you, not you . . .6. . . him."

The miller did not like being laughed at, so he made the donkey start . . .7. . .

Then the boy began to feel tired and the . . .8. . . lifted him onto the donkey's back.

A little further on they . . .9. . . three merchants who were angry when they saw the . . .10. . . riding while the miller walked.

"Why you lazy lad." . . .11. . . said. "Get down from the donkey and let the old . . .12. . . ride."

The miller made the boy get down and he himself . . .13. . . onto the donkey's back. But it was very hot and the boy soon became . . .14. . . again.

After a while they met three girls. "Shame . . .15. . . you master," they called out. "How can you ride at ease, while your . . .16. . . son limps so wearily behind?"

The Miller, the Boy and the Donkey
Brian Wildsmith

The traffic lights

Here is a description of traffic waiting at the traffic lights.

Read the description. Then draw a picture of the scene. (You will probably need two or three attempts before you get your picture just right.)

It is raining very hard. The sky is grey, with four clouds blacker than the rest of the sky. The traffic lights at the very edge of your picture are on red and there is a long queue of traffic waiting. First there is a big, blue car with a long aerial and shiny black tyres. Just behind it is a lorry with the words 'Sand and Cement' on its side. In between the lorry and a little green car is a motorcycle. The rider is wearing a red helmet and a bright yellow suit. The last vehicle is a big red bus. It is full of people.

There is a policeman standing next to the lorry. He is talking to the lorry driver. Behind the bus is a zebra crossing and waiting to cross is a mother with two small children. The children are wearing blue raincoats and hats. Mum carries a blue umbrella.

When you think you have got your picture right, check it again. Make sure the colours are right and the traffic in the correct order. What do you think the policeman and the lorry driver are saying to each other?

What happens next?

Here are the beginnings of some stories. Read them, and decide how you think the stories might end. Then draw a picture to show the ending of your story.

A   One day Jane was walking down the street swinging her bag. She saw an old lady outside a greengrocer's shop, looking at the fruit and vegetables set out on the pavement. Just then she heard the sound of a go-cart coming up behind her. . .

1 Who do you think was in the go-cart?
2 Do you think the old lady heard it?
3 Write what you think happens next and how the story ends.

B   The children in Mrs Smith's class were getting dressed after P.E. Most children were ready, but not all of them. Mrs Smith held up a vest. One child still had bare feet and was holding a sock. . .

1 What do you think Mrs Smith was saying?
2 What do you think the child was saying?
3 Write what you think happens next and how the story ends.

C   Mary said she would help her mother and do the washing-up. She put all the pots and pans in the sink and turned on the hot water. As she added the washing-up liquid the bottle slipped out of her hand and fell into the water. Then she found that she couldn't turn off the tap. . .

1 What happened to the washing-up liquid in the water?
2 How do you think Mary felt?
3 Write what you think happens next and how the story ends.

D   Jim liked going to the supermarket with his mother. One day he was sitting in the shopping trolley as his mother pushed it along. They came to a part where cans were piled up. Then Jim's mother turned to talk to a friend. Jim felt the trolley moving away. . .

1 Where was the trolley heading?
2 What do you think happened next?
3 Write an ending to the story.

Kofi and the eagle

Kofi has brought home a baby eagle. He plans to keep it until it is big and then sell it for a lot of money. But first they have to get it to eat. . .

Ama brought some grains of cooked rice. "Here," she said, "here, let's try some of this."

Kofi made a smooth place in the sand and lifted the baby eagle out of the basket. Ama put grains of cooked rice on
5 her finger and held it out to the baby eagle. It opened its pink curved beak and pecked and Ama pushed the rice inside. But the puffy white rice stuck in its throat. It could not swallow it and it wouldn't open its beak again.

"Come on," said Ama. "It is nice. It is good stuff." But
10 the baby eagle turned its head away.

"He doesn't like it," said Kofi. "The zoo man said he needed raw meat."

"Where can we get raw meat?" said Ama. They gazed at the baby eagle in silence. Its eyes were closed in the glare
15 from the hot sand.

"He doesn't like the sun," said Ama. "A baby that size should not be out of doors at all. He is too young. His sky family will call him back."

Ama sprang up. "We must make a shady house for him."
20 Kofi turned the basket on its side and they laid big green banana leaves across it. Inside the baby eagle pressed itself against the back of the basket away from the children.

"He is unhappy," said Ama. "He wants his mother and his own nest."
25 "Let's make him a nest," said Kofi.

They collected palm fronds and grass, lifting their feet

high as they ran because the sand scorched their soles. They tucked the grass in a circle round the baby eagle. It gazed out at them from its nest with its eyes half-closed, like tiny crescent moons.

30

"He likes his nest," said Ama, "and he wants to sleep. Babies sleep most of the day," she whispered.

"If only he would eat. . ." said Kofi.

Kofi and the Eagle
Geraldine Kaye

1 How did Ama try to feed the baby eagle?
2 Why couldn't it eat the rice?
3 What did the zoo man say eagles eat? How do you think baby eagles get their food in the wild?
4 Why did the eagle press to the back of the basket?
5 What four reasons can you find in the passage for why the eagle was unhappy?
6 How did Kofi feel about the eagle? What was he feeling when he said 'If only he would eat. . .'?
7 What do you think Kofi should do with the baby eagle?
8 Have you ever helped look after a baby animal? Write about what it looked like, what it felt like, what it did, how you felt about it.

Frogs, toads and newts

Frogs, toads and newts spend most of their time on land, hidden away in places where it is safe and damp. In the spring they return to the pond to lay their eggs. Frogs lay their eggs in great masses, rather like bunches of grapes. Toads lay long strings of eggs. Newts lay their eggs singly, and stick them to the leaves of underwater plants.

The eggs hatch into tiny, wriggling tadpoles. At first they have no legs at all. After several weeks legs begin to grow: in frogs and toads the back legs appear first; in newt tadpoles the front legs are the first to grow. After three to four months the tadpoles are fully grown and able to leave the pond.

Frogs, toads and newts feed on almost any small creatures they can catch. Newts seize their food in their teeth and gulp it down. Frogs and toads use their tongues to catch food. The tongue is sticky, and divided at the tip. When the frog or toad spots a small creature it shoots out its tongue at high speed. The sticky tip curls round the food, which is carried back to the mouth and swallowed.

1 When do frogs, toads and newts go back to the pond? Why?
2 Why do you not often see these creatures on land?
3 What do you notice about the back legs of frogs and toads compared with their front ones?
4 In what three ways are newts different from frogs and toads?
5 Explain in your own words how frogs and toads catch their food.
6 Why do you think newts stick their eggs to underwater plants?
7 Do you think it is cruel that frogs, toads and newts live by eating smaller creatures? Why?
8 Draw and colour your own picture of one of the creatures in the passage.
9 Now write about your creature. Either:
  (a) write a true story, using the facts in the passage
  (b) write a made-up adventure story about your creature.

Juster and Waiter

Here is a poem with the lines mixed up. Read it, then decide the order the lines should be in to make sense. Write out your order, using the letters at the side of each piece.

A and I'd say, 'Just a minute, Mum'
and my brother'd say
'Wait a minute, Mum'

B My mum had nicknames for me and my brother.
One of us she called Waiter
and the other she called Juster

C 'There you go again' – she'd say
'Juster and Waiter'.

D It started like this:
She'd say, 'Lend me a hand with the washing up
will you, you two?'

Michael Rosen

1 Why do you think the children said what they did?
2 What do you think of Mum in the poem? Was she
  (a) having a bit of fun?
  (b) getting cross?
  (c) very used to what the children said?

The dinosaur

Now try the same with these lines.

A I stayed after school to finish his head
  'He looks quite real' the teacher said

B We made a dinosaur today
  With paper, and paint, and modelling clay

C As she shut the door, and in the room
  there was nothing but me, the monster and gloom

D We made a dinosaur today;
  But now I wish he'd go away!

E He's very big, much bigger than me,
  with purple eyes that seem to see

The poem begins **B** — — — —

1 Why did the child want the dinosaur to go away?
2 Do you think the teacher was pleased with the model? Why?
3 The child stayed on after school to finish the head. What does this tell us about the child and what she was doing?
4 How would you make a model of a dinosaur? Draw and colour a picture of the model you would make.
5 Do you like this poem? Why?

Rescuing the cat

Mary had a pet cat called Uriah. The man who owned Mary's house was cruel. He said the cat was badly behaved and locked it away in a lonely room. The next day he was going to send it to a cats' home. Mary and her friends planned to rescue Uriah. . .

It's only me, Uriah dear, I've come to save you.

The plan was to put Uriah into a cat-basket with the

You won't be inside for long. I promise.

lid firmly fastened down, and to lower him out of the window on a long rope,

to the boys who would be
waiting in the yard below.

Uriah was very
pleased to see Mary
but he didn't much
care for the cat-basket.
    At last he was safely inside.

miaow!

It's Too Frightening for Me
Shirley Hughes

1 Where were the boys waiting?
2 How was the basket to reach the boys?
3 What did Mary promise Uriah? Do you think the cat believed her? Why?
4 How did Mary know that Uriah was glad to see her?
5 Write out the words that tell you:
    (a) what Uriah thought about the cat basket;
    (b) that Mary found it hard to get him in.
6 How would you have got the cat into the basket?
7 Make up another title for the passage.
8 What do you think happens next in the story?

Jack in the castle

Do you know this story? Jack and his mother are very poor. Jack has to sell their last cow to make money. But instead he sells the cow for some magic beans. His mother is very cross. She throws the beans out of the window. When Jack wakes next morning the beans have grown into a tall beanstalk, reaching into the sky. Jack climbs the beanstalk and finds himself in a strange land. He finds a huge castle. . .

Now read on. Some words are missed out of the story. Choose the word which you think fits the story best. Write down the number of the space, and put the word you have chosen next to it.

Jack set off and soon he was standing at the huge gates of a . . .*1*. . . Jack knocked at the door and a tall bony . . .*2*. . . put out her head.

"Good evening" said Jack. "Could you be so . . .*3*. . . as to give me some supper?"

"Supper you want, is it?" said the . . .*4*. . . woman. "It's supper you'll be if you don't hurry away . . .*5*. . . here. My man is a giant Ogre and there's nothing he likes . . .*6*. . . than boys to eat. He'll soon be here."

"Oh! please give me something to . . .*7*. . . I've not had a morsel since yesterday morning."

Well the Ogre's . . .*8*. . . wasn't so bad after all. She took Jack into the . . .*9*. . . and gave him some bread, cheese and a jug of . . .*10*. . . Jack had scarcely started to eat his supper when thump, . . .*11*. . ., thump! The floor began to tremble with the noise of the . . .*12*. . . footsteps.

"Good gracious me, it's my . . .13. . ." said the woman. "Come quick and jump in here." And she bundled . . .14. . . into the oven, just as the giant came into . . .15. . .

He was a big one, to be sure. And he . . .16. . . angry. He began to shout.

"Fee-fi-fo-fum
I smell the blood of an Englishman
Be he alive or be he dead,
I'll grind his bones to spice my bread."

Jack and the Beanstalk
William Stobbs

1 Why didn't the Ogre's wife want Jack to come into the castle?
2 How was the Ogre's wife kind to Jack?
3 How do you think Jack felt as he lay in the oven?
4 Find these words in the story. Write down each word and its meaning in the passage.
    huge   morsel   scarcely   tremble   spice
    bundle
5 Draw a picture of the strange land Jack found at the top of the beanstalk.
6 Finish off the story for yourself. You can either
    (a) Write in your own words how the story of Jack and the Beanstalk ends.
    (b) Make up your own ending for the story.

Alistair's Elephant

Alistair is a very busy little boy. He works hard at school, and every Saturday he goes to the Zoo. One Saturday an elephant follows him home. . .

"You can't keep him", shouted his mother from the bedroom window. Alistair didn't want to. He didn't have time for a pet. So he called the Zoo Keeper and the Zoo Keeper checked his records. There was a hippopotamus
5   missing, but not an elephant.

"Are you sure it's not a hippo?" he asked. Alistair was certain.

The elephant didn't leave that night, nor any night that week. Alistair had a very hard time sleeping with the
10   elephant at his window.

On Saturday Alistair took the elephant back to the Zoo. He didn't have time for an elephant every day of the week. The Zoo Keeper checked his records and found a mistake. He had been missing an elephant after all. He thanked
15   Alistair very much. The elephant was very sad. Alistair was a little sad too, but he promised the elephant he would visit every Saturday. Then Alistair left for home. It had been a busier than usual week and, at times, it had been fun but he was very happy to be going home to his quiet, tidy room
20   where, at last. . .

Alistair's Elephant
Roger Bollen and Marilyn Sadler

1 What did the Zoo Keeper think was missing from his Zoo when Alistair called him?
2 Why didn't Alistair want to keep the elephant?
3 Write in your own words what happened when Alistair went back to the Zoo the week after.
4 Why do you think the elephant was sad?
5 Why was Alistair looking forward to going home at the end?
6 Look at the picture. How do you think Alistair will feel when he turns round?
7 Write down two good things you could do if you had an elephant as a pet.
8 What problems might there be in having a pet elephant? Draw a picture of one of these problems.

Where the flowers went

Where have all the flowers gone,
The flowers that were standing on
The grave beside the churchyard wall?
  My little brother grabbed them

And stuffed them in an old tin can
And took them home to give my Gran,
Who wasn't very pleased at all –
  'Tell me where you nabbed them!'

  Then out we crept
  As quiet as mice
  To put them back
  Without being caught:

  'It's wrong,' said Gran,
  'But still the thought
  Was
  Nice!'

From: *Hot Dog and Other Poems*
Kit Wright

1 Where did little brother get the flowers?
2 What did he do with them?
3 Why do you think Gran wasn't pleased?
4 Why do you think they put the flowers back?
5 Do you think little brother meant to do wrong?
6 What did Gran mean at the end?
7 Pick out pairs of words at the end of lines which rhyme
  (sound the same) like 'wall, all' . . . See if you can find
  three sets of words.

Babbling and gabbling

Here's another poem about a Granny. Read it through and talk about the funny words like 'corker, cracker, yackety yacker'. Why do you think the writer uses words like these? Now see if you can answer the questions below.

My Granny's an absolute corker,
My Granny's an absolute cracker,
But she's Britain's speediest talker
And champion yackety-yacker!

Everyone's fond of my Granny,
Everyone thinks she's nice,
But before you can say Jack Robinson,
My Granny's said it twice!

From: *Hot Dog and Other Poems*
Kit Wright

1 What do you think Granny is best at?
2 What do people think about Granny?
3 Write about your perfect Granny. What would she be good at? What would people say about her?
4 Draw a picture of your own Granny or your made-up Granny.
5 Look at the words at the ends of the lines. Which ones *rhyme* (sound the same)? Now see if you can write four lines about your Granny using words that sound the same at the end of the lines.

Sharks

*Pat is a young sea otter who never stops asking questions.
Her friend Bobby often gives her the answers. In this part of
the story Pat learns how dangerous hungry sharks can be.*

"I want to ask you about sharks."

"There's no time. Quick. On your tummy. Follow me.
No, come beside me."

"Why?" Pat said.

5   "Save your breath and come as fast as you can to the
beach, and then we're going to climb onto the beach.
There are sharks behind us. Don't look. Just keep moving.
Fast."

So Pat did. They scrambled onto the sand and lolloped
10 up the beach.

"Now", said Bobby. "Turn round and look."

Pat did. There were fins sticking up in the water, and they
could see tails lashing about.

"Well, I didn't mean you to learn about sharks quite like
15 that. They can swim faster than us but they can't come on
land, so if you see a shark coming near you the best thing is
to get to a beach or on rocks, as quickly as you can."

"But we can't stay on land very long," Pat said, "It isn't
good for our fur."

20   "Oh, they'll soon go away. They're cross at the moment
because they didn't catch us but they'll move off and then
we can go back."

The Otter Who Wanted to Know
Jill Tomlinson

1 What could Pat and Bobby see as they looked towards the sea?
2 Why did the otters swim to the beach?
3 Why couldn't the otters stay on land for long?
4 Who do you think asks about the sharks at the beginning of the passage?
5 Why do you think the sharks chased the otters?
6 Why do you think Bobby told Pat 'Save your breath' (line 5) and 'Don't look' (line 7)?
7 What made Bobby think the sharks were cross?
8 How can rocks in the sea be useful to otters?
9 If you could ask the otters a question about life in the sea, what would it be?
10 What do you think will happen next in the story?

Find the title

The story below does not have a title. Read it carefully. Then think up a title of your own for the story.

Going to school Patsy was pulling on her Mum's arm. Why couldn't she hurry up?

Why did she have to stop to look in the shop window! She could do that on the way back. Why was she waiting for Mrs Smith?

"Doesn't she know it's my day to feed the class hamster and clean out his cage?"

That's why Patsy was in a hurry. She knew that she would be able to go into school before the bell rang and get the job done. Then she would have a few minutes to play with Hammy all by herself before the others came in. She would be able to feel his cold feet and twitching nose on her hand and perhaps she would be brave enough to let him crawl around her neck like he did with Jenny.

"Oh, come on Mum."

1 Why did Patsy's Mum stop?
2 What was Patsy's job for the day?
3 What does the passage tell us about hamsters?
4 Find a picture of a hamster and copy it carefully. Give your hamster a name.
5 In your own words, explain why Patsy was in such a hurry to get to school.

Now do the same for this story.

Jimmy couldn't find one of his new football socks anywhere. It was a red one with a white top, just like the ones United wear. They were Jimmy's favourite team. He went to watch them with his Dad. Jimmy looked everywhere but still he couldn't find the sock. Just then he heard a loud voice from the garden.

"Hey Jimmy, what's this doing here behind this bush?" It was Dad, holding up a dirty-looking red and white sock.

"It wasn't me," said Jimmy, "how did it get there?"

Then he saw a movement in the bush. It was his dog Spot, creeping away with his tail between his legs.

Which of these titles fits the story best?
> Come On United
> Spot Steals the Sock
> The Search
> Dad in the Garden.

Now make up a title of your own.

1 Why do you think Spot was creeping away?
2 How do you think Jimmy felt when he couldn't find his football sock?
3 What do you think his Dad thought when he found the sock?
4 Draw a picture of either:
   (a) Jimmy wearing a United football strip
   (b) Someone wearing your favourite team's football strip.

Oh, that's ridiculous

Vegetables

Eat a tomato and you'll turn red
(I don't think that's really so);
Eat a carrot and you'll turn orange
(Still and all you never know);
Eat some spinach and you'll turn green
(I'm not saying that it's true
But that's what I heard, and so
I thought I'd pass it on to you).

Shel Silverstein

Down the stream the swans all glide

Down the stream the swans all glide;
It's quite the cheapest way to ride.
Their legs get wet,
Their tummies wetter:
I think after all
The bus is better.

Spike Milligan
From Oh That's Ridiculous

1 Draw, colour and label the fruits and vegetables in the first poem.

2 Make up three lines of your own like the ones in the first poem:

   Eat a .... and you'll ....

3 Do you think the writer of the first poem really believes that eating vegetables makes you change colour?

4 Make a list of the vegetables you don't like to eat. Now make a list of the ones you do like. Draw a picture of the vegetable you like best, and label it.

5 Look at the second poem again. What are the swans gliding on? Draw a picture about the poem.

6 Would a bus be a good way to travel where the swans travel? If not, why not?

7 Draw a picture of your favourite way of travelling.

8 Write a poem or story of your own about swans. Try to use words that describe their colour and shape.

9 Look carefully at both poems. Some words at the ends of the lines *rhyme* (sound the same). Write down the pairs of words which sound alike.

Fox eyes

The fox was a spy, he spied on the opossums, who were supposed to be asleep, on a rabbit, who froze like a statue, on a squirrel hiding his nuts, on a bear hiding his honey, on a fat, little dog burying her bone and, finally, some children who were supposed to be taking a nap in the afternoon and weren't sleeping at all.

"Whiskerchew!" the fox coughed. And the children knew the fox knew that they were not sleeping. All this the fox noted, and he went on his way. But that night there was pandemonium among the animals. That night the opos-
5 sums didn't play possum. The rabbit ran around all night. The squirrel got excited and ate all his nuts. The little fat dog dug up her bone. And the bear ate all his honey. And the children who were supposed to be sleeping were not sleepy.
10 But the fox just yawned. He sighed and he yawned. Then he lowered his ears, curled his big, bushy tail around him, closed his eyes, and went to sleep. He went to sleep right away without even thinking about what he had seen. For, of course, the fox could never remember the next day what
15 he had seen the day before.
But no one knows that but the fox.

Fox Eyes
M.W. Brown and G. Williams

1 Make a list of everyone the fox spied on.
2 Why do you think the rabbit froze?
3 Who did the fox see hiding things?
4 Why do you think there was pandemonium among the animals that night?
5 Who didn't 'play possum' (line 5)? What do you think this means?
6 What did the squirrel and the bear do during the night?
7 Why do you think the children stayed awake?
8 In your own words, write down what the fox did that night.
9 Look at the last two lines of the story. Should the children and animals have been worried about what the fox saw? If not, why not?
10 Why do you think the story is called 'Fox Eyes'? Do you think this is a good title? Think of another title for the story.

Festivals

Festivals are special days or times in the year, like Christmas, Bonfire Night and Halloween, when we do things we don't do at any other time. Here are three different festivals celebrated by people who live in Britain.

Eid-ul-Fitr

Eid-ul-Fitr is a great day in the Muslim religion. Most of the Muslim people who live in Britain today come from Pakistan or Arab countries. The festival comes in June or July. It marks the end of Ramadan, a month of fasting, when Muslims go without food during the daytime. On this special day people get up early and say their morning prayers. Then they put on new clothes and go to the Mosque for prayer. At Eid, Muslims send cards to their friends, give presents, and eat sweets, dates and special food.

Chinese New Year

The Chinese New Year or Spring Festival comes sometime between 20 January and 20 February. At this time Chinese people decorate their homes, cook special meals, go to visit friends and enjoy themselves. The holiday colour is red, which is the colour of happiness. Small red envelopes, called 'ang pow', are given to children. They contain sweets, money or small presents. The New Year festival lasts for two weeks. At the end there is a Lantern Festival, which is celebrated with music and dancing. The most popular dance is the Dragon Dance, when people dress up in dragon costumes.

Diwali

Diwali is the Indian New Year festival. It is celebrated by Hindu people in November. Hinduism is the main religion of India. Diwali is also called the Festival of Lights. Houses and shops are decorated with lamps and brightly-coloured lights. People send out Diwali greetings cards and presents, and eat Diwali cakes and sweets. Sometimes fireworks are set off, and there is always plenty of music and dancing.

Copy out this chart on a big piece of paper and fill it in. See if you can put in the information about Christmas for yourself.

	Date of the festival	Who celebrates it?	What do people do?	What do children get?
Eid-ul-Fitr				
Chinese New Year				
Diwali				
Christmas				

1 What things are the same in all the festivals?
2 Draw a picture showing what happens at one of the festivals in the passages.
3 Draw a picture of another special time, and write about what happens then.

The garden

"A Princess is coming to visit our country," said Lion. "Now how can we show her how happy we are to see her?"

"We could bow very low, and smile," said Hippo. "But some of us aren't the right shape for bowing, and smiling isn't enough by itself."

"We could show the Princess how fast we can run," said Giraffe.

"Or jump!" added Grasshopper. "But some of us aren't very good at running or jumping."

"We could cheer," said Porcupine.

"Or trumpet!" added Elephant. "But perhaps the Princess would be frightened."

"We could dance," said Secretary Bird.

Lion looked at Hippo and tried to imagine him dancing. He shook his head, and the animals stared at each other and sighed.

Small Brown Bird, who had listened quietly, opened his beak and chirruped shyly: "Couldn't we make a garden, Lion? Princesses love flowers."

Everyone stared at Small Brown Bird.

"That's quite a good idea," said Lion. "We can all help to make a garden."

First, the animals chose a piece of land.

"But it's much too rough," said Lion. "We must break up those big, hard lumps of earth."

"I will do that," cried Hippo at once. "My feet are large and my body is heavy." He stamped on the earth with his big feet, until it was smooth and fine.

"Good!" said Lion. "Now we must make some tiny holes in which to plant the flower seeds."

"I will do that," Porcupine cried. "The spines on my back are very sharp." He curled himself into a prickly ball, and rolled over and over the earth until it was covered with tiny holes.

"Good!" said Lion. "Now we must plant the seeds."

"I will do that," Grasshopper cried. "I am light and quick."

From *The Anita Hewett Animal Story Book*

1 How many animals are there in the story? Write down their names.
2 Whose idea is it to welcome the Princess?
3 Why do you think Giraffe suggests running and Elephant trumpeting?
4 Why is Secretary Bird's idea not a good one?
5 Who has the best idea of all?
6 How does Hippo help make the garden?
7 What job do you think Elephant could do to help the plants grow?
8 There are two more jobs to do:
   (a) someone must keep watch so that Monkey does not spoil the garden;
   (b) someone must weed the garden.
Which job do you think Giraffe would be best at? Why?
Can you think of any more jobs that might need doing?

First published in 1985 by Basil Blackwell Limited
Reprinted 1988, 1989, 1991

Reprinted in 1992, 1993, 1994 by Simon & Schuster Education

This edition published by
Stanley Thornes (Publishers) Ltd
Ellenborough House
Wellington Street
CHELTENHAM GL50 1YW
England
98 99 00/10 9 8 7 6 5 4

A catalogue record for this book is available from the British Library.

ISBN 0 7487 1965 2

Acknowledgements

We are grateful to the following for permission to reproduce copyright material: Associated Book Publishers Ltd for 'The Beech Tree' from Oh Really Rabbit! by Ruth Manning-Sanders, for 'Sharks' from The Otter Who Wanted to Know by Jill Tomlinson, and for an extract from Kofi and the Eagle by Geraldine Kaye; The Bodley Head for 'The Garden' from The Anita Hewett Animal Story Book by Anita Hewett; Jonathan Cape Ltd for 'The wormy spaghetti' from The Twits by Roald Dahl; William Rossa Cole for 'Vegetables' by Shel Silverstein; Collins Publishers for extracts from Fox Eyes by Margaret Wise Brown, and from Penny and the Captain by J. B. Zalben; Andre Deutsch Ltd for 'Juster and Waiter' from You Can't Catch Me by Michael Rosen; Hamish Hamilton Ltd for an extract from Alistair's Elephant by Roger Bollen and Marilyn Sadler; Hodder and Stoughten Ltd for an extract from It's Too Frightening for Me by Shirley Hughes; Spike Milligan Productions Ltd for Down the Stream by Spike Milligan; Oxford University Press for an extract from The Miller, the Boy and the Donkey by Brian Wildsmith; Penguin Books Ltd for 'Where the flowers went' and 'Babbling and Gabbling' from Hot Dog and Other Poems by Kit Wright, and for an extract from Jack and the Beanstalk by William Stobbs.

Typesetting by Getset (BTS) Ltd, Eynsham, Oxford

Printed in Hong Kong by Wing King Tong Co. Ltd.

48